# Dear Parent:
## Your child's love of reading starts here!

Every child learns to read in a different way and at his or her own speed. Some go back and forth between reading levels and read favorite books again and again. Others read through each level in order. You can help your young reader improve and become more confident by encouraging his or her own interests and abilities. From books your child reads with you to the first books he or she reads alone, there are I Can Read Books for every stage of reading:

### SHARED READING
Basic language, word repetition, and whimsical illustrations, ideal for sharing with your emergent reader

### BEGINNING READING
Short sentences, familiar words, and simple concepts for children eager to read on their own

### READING WITH HELP
Engaging stories, longer sentences, and language play for developing readers

### READING ALONE
Complex plots, challenging vocabulary, and high-interest topics for the independent reader

### ADVANCED READING
Short paragraphs, chapters, and exciting themes for the perfect bridge to chapter books

**I Can Read Books** have introduced children to the joy of reading since 1957. Featuring award-winning authors and illustrators and a fabulous cast of beloved characters, I Can Read Books set the standard for beginning readers.

A lifetime of discovery begins with the magical words **"I Can Read!"**

*Visit www.icanread.com for information*
*on enriching your child's reading experience.*

Pete the Cat: Sir Pete the Brave
Copyright © 2016 by James Dean
All rights reserved. Printed in the United States of America. No part of this book may be used or reproduced in any manner whatsoever
without written permission except in the case of brief quotations embodied in critical articles and reviews. For information address
HarperCollins Children's Books, a division of HarperCollins Publishers, 195 Broadway, New York, NY 10007.
www.icanread.com

ISBN 978-0-06-240422-0 (trade bdg.) — ISBN 978-0-06-240421-3 (pbk.)

16  17  18  19  20   LSCC   10 9 8 7 6 5 4 3      ❖      First Edition

I Can Read!

SHARED
My First
READING

# Pete the Cat
## SIR PETE THE BRAVE

by
James Dean

HARPER
*An Imprint of HarperCollinsPublishers*

Meet Sir Pete,
the bravest knight
in the land!

Sir Pete rides a horse
and climbs towers.

At dinner, Sir Pete listens
to Lady Callie play the harp.
Lady Callie is awesome!

"Bravo!" Sir Pete yells
at the end of each song.
He claps louder than anyone.

One night, while Lady Callie
plays beautifully,
someone casts a spell.

And everyone falls asleep—
even Sir Pete!

The next morning,
Lady Callie is gone!
"Oh no!" says Sir Pete
the Brave.

"I will find Lady Callie
and save her."
"Giddyup!"

Sir Pete falls in a hole!
The hole is a
dragon's footprint!

"Follow the footprints!"
Sir Pete says to his horse.

The footprints stop!

Where did the dragon go?

Sir Pete looks up . . .

. . . and sees the dragon
flying across the lake with
Lady Callie and her harp!

Sir Pete can't fly,

but he can row.

Across the lake he goes!

Sir Pete sees a dragon cave!
He has to go inside,
but it is very dark.

Then he hears music.

He must save Lady Callie.

He won't be scared.

He finds a harp.

But no Lady Callie.

Sir Pete will not give up.

He climbs the highest hill.

He looks around for Lady
Callie.

Then he hears a loud growl.

Sir Pete is scared.

# The hill starts to move!

Sir Pete is on the
dragon's back!

Sir Pete knows what to do!
He slides down, down, down
the dragon's back.

The dragon sees Pete and roars!
"Sir Pete!" says Lady Callie.
"I will save you!"

"Save me?"

says Sir Pete.

"But I came to save you."

Sir Pete and Lady Callie
start to argue.
The dragon starts to cry.

"I just wanted to sing along."

The dragon sobs.

"I did not want to hurt anyone."

"I have an idea!" says Sir Pete.
"Will you give us a lift?"

The dragon flies Sir Pete
and Lady Callie home.
Everyone is happy to see them.

"You don't need a great
voice to make music,"
says Sir Pete. "Just good
friends!"

The dragon joins the song.
Three cheers for Lady Callie
and for Sir Pete the Brave!